An Encyclopedia of Embroidery Stitches

by Jane Cannon Meyers

Bobbie Matela, Managing Editor
Carol Wilson Mansfield, Art Director
Carly Poggemeyer, Editorial Director
Jane Cannon Meyers, Senior Editor
Pam Nichols, Editor
Mary Hernandez, Illustrations and Book Design

Photographed examples were stitched by:
Linda Causee and Jane Meyers.

For a full-color catalog including books of needlework designs, write to:

American School of Needlework®, Consumer Division
1455 Linda Vista Drive, San Marcos, CA 92069

We have made every effort to ensure the accuracy and completeness of these instructions.

We cannot, however, be responsible for human error, typographical mistakes, or variations in individual work.

ISBN:0-88195-921-9   Printed in U.S.A.   All rights reserved.   5 6 7 8 9

Introduction

Here is a book that will increase your confidence and enjoyment as an embroiderer. We've included 101 stitches and illustrated each and every one on both evenweave fabric and plain weave fabric.

On pages 9 to 12 you'll find each stitch photographed in full color for a beautiful presentation that will quickly let you view all 101 stitches. The stitches are first shown as surface embroidery (pages 9 and 10) and then repeated on evenweave fabric (pages 11 and 12).

Leaf through pages 14 to 67 and you'll find each stitch clearly illustrated along with a step-by-step explanation of how to work the stitch as surface embroidery and on evenweave fabric.

Whether you are an experienced or beginning embroiderer, whether you embroider regularly or occasionally, you are sure to find this book a reliable reference for many years.

Table of Contents

Surface Stitchery and Evenweave Embroidery
What is the difference?

The terms Surface Stitchery and Evenweave Embroidery actually describe the type of fabric on which embroidery is worked, rather than the type of stitch that is used. The fabrics for Surface Stitchery can be any stitchable surface, such as cotton, linen, silk, wool or synthetics; felt, velvet, or terrycloth; twill weave or plain weave, etc. If it is of a weight and weave through which one can pull a needle and appropriate thread, we call it a stitchable surface. The name of the stitch (e.g., Cross Stitch, Stem Stitch, Satin Stitch) is the same regardless of the type of fabric used.

The embroiderer can choose a variety of threads for both kinds of needlework. For Surface Stitchery, one can make stitches of differing sizes and vary their placement. On the other hand, Evenweave Embroidery is worked on a fabric or canvas that has the same number of threads woven horizontally and vertically within a measured space. The size and placement of the stitches are confined to that weave.

The fiber content of evenweave fabrics can vary considerably and also the number of threads per inch. The number of threads per inch is referred to as the fabric's thread count. When embroidering stitches on an evenweave, the stitches will be worked over a specific number of threads, so you do not have the freedom to alter the size of the stitches—that was determined when you chose your fabric. The thread count of the evenweave will also determine what threads can be used for proper coverage of the surface without distortion of the fabric.

A few words about stitch names. Many of these 101 embroidery stitches have several different names. Sometimes a name is associated with a geographical area or a period of history, or it may be described by construction method. Different reference books often list a variety of other names. We have chosen the most common name for each stitch, with illustrations for working the stitch on plain surfaces and evenweaves.

The stitches are presented alphabetically on pages 14-67 with an index on page 68. The color pages 9-12 show all the stitches worked on both surfaces. The covers have beautifully used many of the stitches.

Embroidery Supplies
What do I need?

Fabrics
An array of different fabrics that are commonly used for surface stitchery and evenweave embroidery is shown in the photo. Your project and personal taste will determine the fabric and threads to use for a project. One fabric not shown, but with a weave that is even, is Aida cloth, a popular cross stitch surface that has blocks of thread. Many (but not all) of these stitches can be worked on Aida by following the evenweave directions, usually counting two fabric threads as one block of Aida cloth. All evenweave stitches can also be worked on needlepoint canvas.

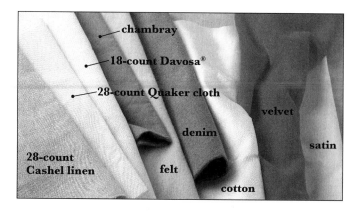

When preparing fabric for embroidery, be sure to cut a large enough piece for your finished project, including whatever margin is needed for finishing. Overcast or machine-zigzag the raw edges to prevent raveling.

Needles
The needles used for embroidery are sharps (with a sharp point) or tapestry (with a blunt point). Needles are sized by number with the highest number being the smallest and thinnest needle. Usually, one of the several kinds of sharps (called embroidery, crewel, sewing, etc.) is used for Surface Stitchery. Tapestry needles are usually used for Evenweave Embroidery or when it is important to stitch between fabric threads without splitting them.

When deciding what size needle to use, choose one that is easy to thread with the amount of thread required, but is not so large that it will leave holes in the fabric.

Cut thread into comfortable working lengths—we suggest about 18". When working with several colors, thread several needles in advance, so they are ready when you want to change colors.

Threads

Until recent years, the favorite thread for embroidery was six-strand cotton floss. It can be divided to work with one, two, or more strands at a time. On our color pages 9-12 we used #8 pearl cotton, one or two strands of cotton floss, and occasional metallic threads for the stitched examples.

In recent years there has been an explosion of wonderful threads with various fiber contents to create a variety of effects. Choose from the threads, shown at right, or any other new ones you might find!

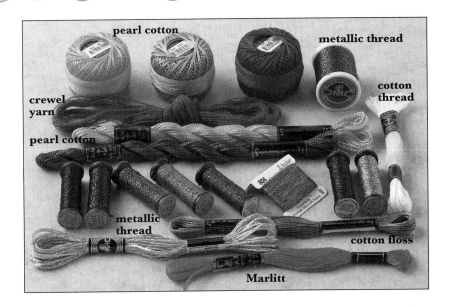

Getting Started
How do I begin and end threads?

To begin an area of work where there is no previous stitching, you can hold an inch of the thread end against the back of the fabric and anchor it with your first few stitches.

You can also begin with one of the following versions of a waste knot. For a Basic Waste Knot, make a small knot at the end of the thread; stitch down into fabric a distance ahead of (and in the path of) your first few stitches with the knot on the surface of the fabric. Bring needle up and work a few stitches, anchoring the thread on the back. When the knot is reached, cut it off.

Basic Waste Knot

For an Away Waste Knot, make a small knot 2" or 3" from your beginning stitch (and away from the working area) so knot is on the surface of the fabric. Bring needle up and work stitches. Later, cut off the waste knot, thread the beginning thread into a needle, and weave it through some completed stitches on the back of the fabric.

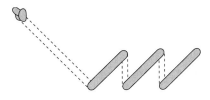

Away Waste Knot

For a Needle Waste Knot, insert one end of thread into a needle and park it away from the working area; it can be secured by wrapping thread around needle once or twice to anchor. Thread opposite end of thread into another needle; stitch down then bring needle up to begin stitching. Later, undo the parked needle, bring thread to back, and weave through the beginning stitches. This is especially helpful when you want the thread to be placed in a certain direction on the back.

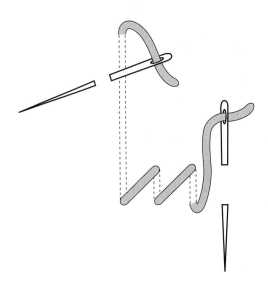

Needle Waste Knot

To finish threads and begin new ones next to existing stitches, weave through the backs of several stitches, preferably of the same color. Do not carry your thread any distance across the back of your work as it may show through to the front.

Hoops and Frames

The use of a hoop or frame to hold your stitching is optional, but it will depend on personal preference and/or choice of fabric. If you like a hoop, choose a clean plastic or wood version with a screw-type tension adjuster. Be sure to remove the hoop when you are not stitching and avoid crushing stitched areas as you progress.

For a large project, a plastic snap-together frame, scroll-type wooden frame, or stretcher bars, will hold your fabric taut throughout the stitching process and help produce smooth, even stitching without distortion of the background fabric.

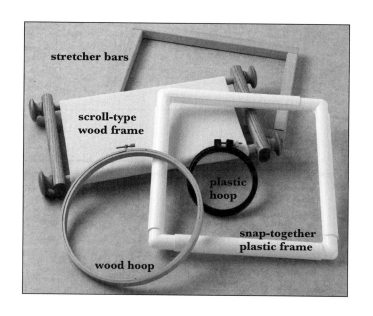

Stitching Tips and Techniques

- When working with stranded threads like floss, always separate the strands then put together and realign the number you wish to use.

- If a needle is difficult to thread, turn it over so you are threading the opposite side of the hole—it may slip in more easily. You can also try inserting the other end of the thread into the needle.

- If you will be working with different colors and kinds of threads, thread each into a needle before beginning your first stitch. Each new color will be readily available when you need it!

- When continuing a stitch with a new piece of the same kind of thread, end the used thread by holding it (or making a waste knot) in the same direction you are working. Weave in the new thread, also in the same direction as you are working to minimize the joined appearance.

- The neatest stitches are achieved by pulling the needle and thread completely through the fabric for each portion of the stitch.

- Strive for consistent tension as you work. If you are trying a new stitch, practice a few rows on scrap fabric to establish a rhythm.

- If a mistake is made, remove the needle from the thread and unpick the work back to the error and restitch. If you try to "unstitch" the work, you'll usually make a mess!

Finishing Notes

Dampen embroidery and place it face down on a dry towel or padded surface; press carefully until dry.

Mount and frame as desired. For a slightly puffy look, add a layer of fleece beneath the embroidery.

How To Use This Book

These embroidery stitches are numbered 1 to 101 and their working directions are presented on pages 14 to 67 in alphabetical order. Many of them are shown slightly reduced on the front and back covers. The front cover schematic is shown below and the back cover schematic is on page 8, and show each stitch identified by its number, not the page number. The cover work is Surface Stitchery using six-strand cotton floss, silk floss, pearl cotton, rayon thread, crewel wool, and metallic threads.

If you wish to re-create the front cover design, use removable ink to trace the outlines of the shapes, refer to the schematic and stitch directions, and use threads and colors of your choice.

On the color pages 9, 10, 11, and 12, you will find color photos of all the stitches worked as Surface Stitchery and Evenweave Embroidery. The directions for making each stitch are accompanied by illustrations. Number 8 pearl cotton, 6-strand cotton embroidery floss, and metallic cord were used for these interior photos.

Before you begin an embroidery project, refer to the color photos when choosing stitches, and if a stitch is new, practice a few until the desired look is achieved.

Front Cover Schematic

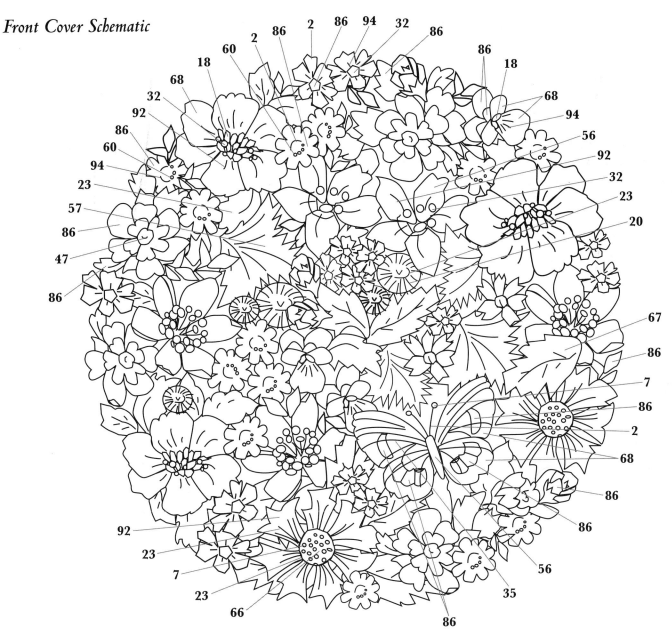

Back Cover Schematic

Each stitch is identified by its number, not the page number.

8

1 Arrowhead Stitch

2 Backstitch

3 Backstitch—Split

4 Backstitch—Threaded

5 Backstitch—Wrapped

6 Basque Knot

7 Bead Stitch

8 Bead Stitch with Cross Stitch

9 Bead St. with Half Cross Stitch

10 Bead St. Worked in a Cradle

11 Blanket Stitch

12 Blanket Stitch—Closed

13 Blanket Stitch—Double

14 Blanket Stitch—Looped

15 Blanket Stitch—Uneven

16 Blanket St.—Up and Down

17 Bosnia Stitch

18 Bullion Knot

19 Buttonhole Stitch

20 Buttonhole Stitch—Circular

21 Buttonhole St.—Scalloped

22 Cable Stitch

23 Chain Stitch

24 Chain Stitch—Braided

25 Chain Stitch—Cable

26 Chain Stitch—Lazy Daisy

27 Chain Stitch—Open

28 Chain Stitch—Rosette

29 Chain Stitch—Twisted

30 Chain Stitch—Zigzag

31 Chevron Stitch

32 Colonial Knot

33 Coral Stitch

34 Coral Stitch—Zigzag

35 Couching

36 Couching—Bokhara

37 Cretan Stitch

38 Cretan Stitch—Open

39 Cross Stitch

40 Cross St.—Double Upright

41 Cross Stitch—Long-Arm

42 Cross Stitch—Oblong

43 Cross Stitch—Reversible

44 Cross Stitch—Smyrna

45 Cross Stitch—Tied

46 Cross Stitch—Upright

47 Eyelet Stitch

48 Eyelet Stitch—Algerian

49 Eyelet Stitch—Diamond

50 Eyelet Stitch—Half

51 Feather Stitch

52 Feather Stitch—Chained

53 Feather Stitch—Closed

54 Feather Stitch—Double

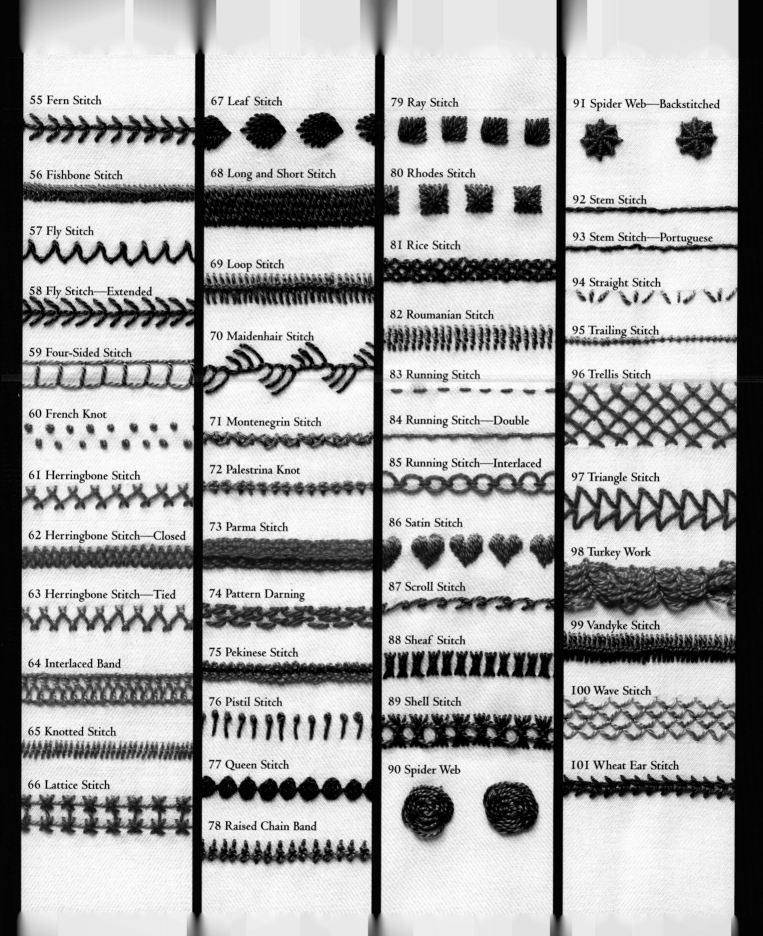

55 Fern Stitch

56 Fishbone Stitch

57 Fly Stitch

58 Fly Stitch—Extended

59 Four-Sided Stitch

60 French Knot

61 Herringbone Stitch

62 Herringbone Stitch—Closed

63 Herringbone Stitch—Tied

64 Interlaced Band

65 Knotted Stitch

66 Lattice Stitch

67 Leaf Stitch

68 Long and Short Stitch

69 Loop Stitch

70 Maidenhair Stitch

71 Montenegrin Stitch

72 Palestrina Knot

73 Parma Stitch

74 Pattern Darning

75 Pekinese Stitch

76 Pistil Stitch

77 Queen Stitch

78 Raised Chain Band

79 Ray Stitch

80 Rhodes Stitch

81 Rice Stitch

82 Roumanian Stitch

83 Running Stitch

84 Running Stitch—Double

85 Running Stitch—Interlaced

86 Satin Stitch

87 Scroll Stitch

88 Sheaf Stitch

89 Shell Stitch

90 Spider Web

91 Spider Web—Backstitched

92 Stem Stitch

93 Stem Stitch—Portuguese

94 Straight Stitch

95 Trailing Stitch

96 Trellis Stitch

97 Triangle Stitch

98 Turkey Work

99 Vandyke Stitch

100 Wave Stitch

101 Wheat Ear Stitch

1 Arrowhead Stitch

2. Backstitch

3. Backstitch—Split

4. Backstitch—Threaded

5. Backstitch—Wrapped

6. Basque Knot

7. Bead Stitch

8. Bead Stitch with Cross Stitch

9. Bead St. with Half Cross Stitch

10. Bead St. Worked in a Cradle

11. Blanket Stitch

12. Blanket Stitch—Closed

13. Blanket Stitch—Double

14. Blanket Stitch—Looped

15. Blanket Stitch—Uneven

16. Blanket St.—Up and Down

17. Bosnia Stitch

18. Bullion Knot

19. Buttonhole Stitch

20. Buttonhole Stitch—Circular

21. Buttonhole Stitch—Scalloped

22. Cable Stitch

23. Chain Stitch

24. Chain Stitch—Braided

25. Chain Stitch—Cable

26. Chain Stitch—Lazy Daisy

27. Chain Stitch—Open

28. Chain Stitch—Rosette

29. Chain Stitch—Twisted

30. Chain Stitch—Zigzag

31. Chevron Stitch

32. Colonial Knot

33. Coral Stitch

34. Coral Stitch—Zigzag

35. Couching

36. Couching—Bokhara

37. Cretan Stitch

38. Cretan Stitch—Open

39. Cross Stitch

40. Cross St.—DoubleUpright

41. Cross Stitch—Long-Arm

42. Cross Stitch—Oblong

43. Cross Stitch—Reversible

44. Cross Stitch—Smyrna

45. Cross Stitch—Tied

46. Cross Stitch—Upright

47. Eyelet Stitch

48. Eyelet Stitch—Algerian

49. Eyelet Stitch—Diamond

50. Eyelet Stitch—Half

51. Feather Stitch

52. Feather Stitch—Chained

53. Feather Stitch—Closed

54. Feather Stitch—Double

EVENWEAVE STITCHES

Fern Stitch to Wheat Ear Stitch •

55 Fern Stitch

56 Fishbone Stitch

57 Fly Stitch

58 Fly Stitch—Extended

59 Four-Sided Stitch

60 French Knot

61 Herringbone Stitch

62 Herringbone Stitch—Closed

63 Herringbone Stitch—Tied

64 Interlaced Band

65 Knotted Stitch

66 Lattice Stitch

67 Leaf Stitch

68 Long and Short Stitch

69 Loop Stitch

70 Maidenhair Stitch

71 Montenegrin Stitch

72 Palestrina Knot

73 Parma Stitch

74 Pattern Darning

75 Pekinese Stitch

76 Pistil Stitch

77 Queen Stitch

78 Raised Chain Band

79 Ray Stitch

80 Rhodes Stitch

81 Rice Stitch

82 Roumanian Stitch

83 Running Stitch

84 Running Stitch—Double

85 Running Stitch—Interlaced

86 Satin Stitch

87 Scroll Stitch

88 Sheaf Stitch

89 Shell Stitch

90 Spider Web

91 Spider Web—Backstitched

92 Stem Stitch

93 Stem Stitch—Portuguese

94 Straight Stitch

95 Trailing Stitch

96 Trellis Stitch

97 Triangle Stitch

98 Turkey Work

99 Vandyke Stitch

100 Wave Stitch

101 Wheat Ear Stitch

The Stitches

Following are step-by-step illustrations for 101 embroidery stitches, each shown on plain fabric (any stitchable surface) and also on evenweave fabric (where the woven threads are counted). Some stitches are variations of a preceding basic stitch.

On plain fabric, shown on the left side of each page, use your judgment for spacing and size of stitches, often working along imaginary guidelines as described. On evenweave fabric, shown on the right side of each page, count the threads as shown for placement of stitches.

When working the stitches from the illustrations, note that the thread that is in progress is shown lighter than the finished portion of the stitch. Refer to the photographs on pages 9 through 12 to view each of the completed stitches.

Unless otherwise noted, bring threaded needle up at 1 and all odd numbers and stitch down at 2 and all even numbers. Finishing stitches or secondary stitching are referred to as A, B, C, etc.

1. Arrowhead Stitch

The Arrowhead Stitch is worked between two imaginary parallel lines. Bring thread up at 1 and stitch down at 2, making a diagonal stitch. Come up at 3 and down at 4, making a diagonal stitch in the opposite direction. Continue in this manner.

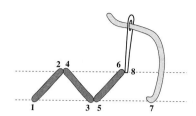

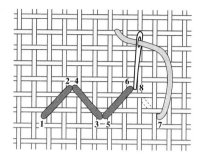

2. Backstitch

Bring thread up at 1, a stitch length from beginning of design line. Stitch down at 2, at beginning of line. Come up at 3, stitch back down at 4 (same hole as 1). Continue in this manner, stitching backward on the surface to meet the previous stitch. Backstitch can be worked horizontally as shown, vertically, diagonally, or along a curve.

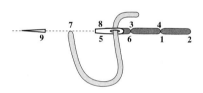

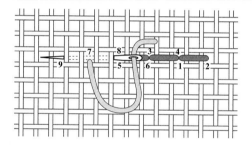

3. Backstitch—Split

Begin as for Backstitch (above), up at 1 down at 2, and up at 3. Stitch down at 4, this time splitting the thread of the first stitch, and come up at 5. Continue in this manner, each time splitting the previous stitch.

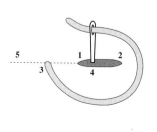

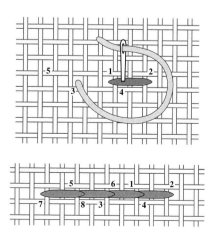

4. Backstitch—Threaded

Work a row of Backstitch (page 14). Bring a matching or contrasting thread up at A, at beginning of line. Pass needle upward beneath first Backstitch, not entering the fabric. Pull through, leaving a loose loop below Backstitch. Pass needle downward in same manner beneath second Backstitch. Repeat to end of backstitch line and stitch down into fabric at B. Keep the loops consistent above and below backstitched line.

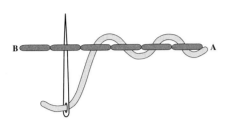

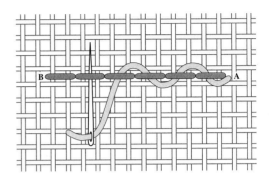

5. Backstitch—Wrapped

Work a row of Backstitch (page 14). Bring a matching or contrasting thread up at A, at beginning of line. Use an overcasting motion to pass needle downward beneath each Backstitch, not entering the fabric. Pull through consistently so each Backstitch is loosely wrapped. Stitch down into fabric at end of backstitched line at B.

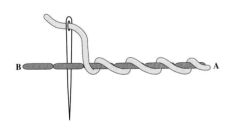

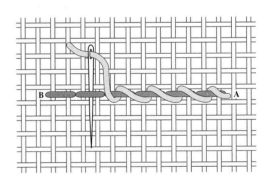

6. Basque Knot

This stitch is worked from right to left along two imaginary parallel lines. Come up at 1, go down at 2 along top line and come back up at 3 (below 1 and even with 2) along bottom line. Swing needle over the top then pass under the first stitch, not entering fabric (A); pull through gently. Make a clockwise loop toward the left. Again swing needle over and under first stitch (B), this time keeping loop beneath point of needle. Pull through gently to form knot. Continue next stitch and subseqent stitches by going down at 4 and up at 5 (same as 2-3 motion) and continuing knot sequence.

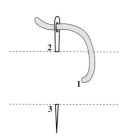

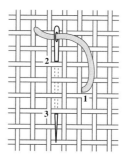

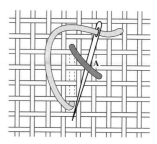

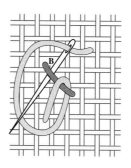

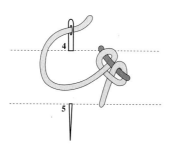

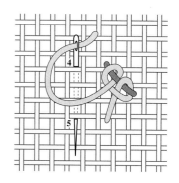

7. Bead Stitch

This traditional method of attaching beads uses a Backstitch (page 14) technique, usually with thread to match the background fabric. Working from right to left, bring thread up at 1, slip on bead, and stitch back down over an intersection of threads at 2. Bring thread forward beneath fabric and come up at 3, slip on bead, and stitch back down at 4. Continue in this manner, anchoring beginning and ending threads well. The beads lie diagonally on the fabric.

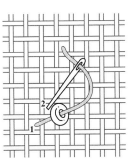

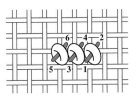

8. Bead Stitch with Cross Stitch

This method attaches beads so they are upright and provides a symmetrical finished surface for a large beaded area. Bring thread up at 1, slip on bead, and stitch down at 2. Bring thread up at 3, stitch through bead, and stitch down at 4 to straighten the bead.

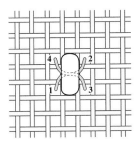

9. Bead Stitch with Half Cross Stitch

A half Cross Stitch can also be used to attach beads, although not as firmly as the Bead Stitch. Working from left to right, bring thread up at 1, slip on bead, and stitch down at 2. Continue in this manner. For added security, stitch twice through each bead. To allow more space between beads, work over every other intersection.

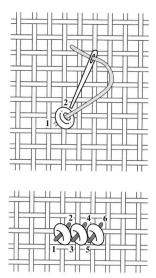

10. Bead Stitch Worked in a Cradle

Use two strands of floss for this method of attachment. Begin as for Bead with Half Cross Stitch (above) and bring thread up at 1, slip on bead, and stitch down at 2. Bring thread up again at 1, separate strands so one is on each side of the bead, forming a cradle to hold bead in place, then stitch down at 2.

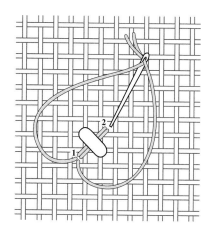

11. Blanket Stitch

This stitch is worked from left to right along two imaginary parallel lines. Bring needle up at 1 and make a counterclockwise loop. Stitch down at 2 (diagonally upward and to the right of 1) and up at 3 (directly below 2), keeping thread beneath point of needle. Pull through downward to form stitch. Continue in this manner, making stitches the same height and evenly spaced. Stitch down over last loop to end row.

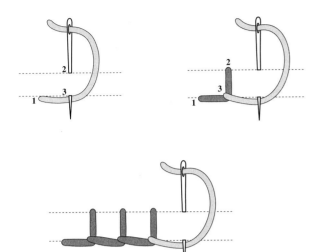

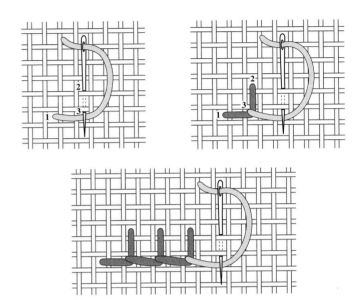

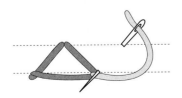

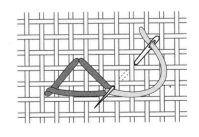

12. Blanket Stitch—Closed

This is a variation of the Blanket Stitch (above) where the tops of two adjacent stitches meet at a point to form a series of triangles. Bring needle up at 1 and make a clockwise loop; stitch down at 2 and up at 3 forming a sloping stitch. Stitch down at 4 (same hole as 2) and up at 5 forming the opposite sloping stitch. Continue in this manner, making triangles the same size.

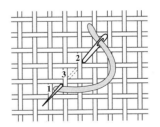

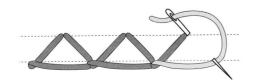

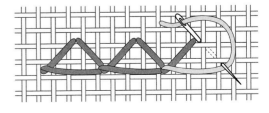

19

13. Blanket Stitch—Double

Two rows of Blanket Stitch are worked so they mesh together with straight edges along the outer sides. Work one row of Blanket Stitch (page 19). Turn fabric top to bottom and work a second row in between the stitches of the first row, but not quite touching. If desired, different colors may be used for each row.

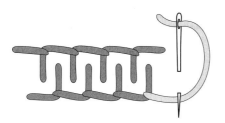

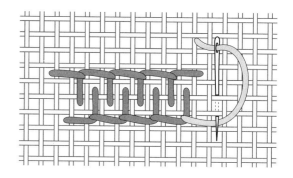

14. Blanket Stitch—Looped

Bring thread up at 1 and loop thread counter-clockwise. Stitch down at 2 and up at 3 with thread beneath point of needle; pull through. Stitch down at 4 to anchor loop and up at 5 (within loop). Repeat sequence for desired length.

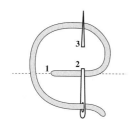

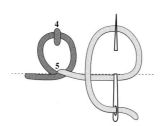

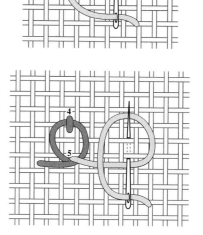

15. Blanket Stitch—Uneven

Begin as for Blanket Stitch (page 19), but make every other stitch half as high as the first stitch.

 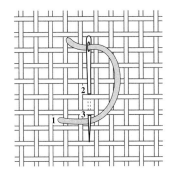

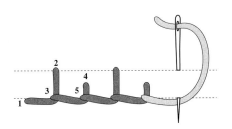 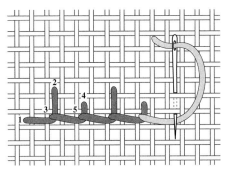

16. Blanket Stitch—Up and Down

Begin as for Blanket Stitch (page 19), coming up at 1, down at 2, and up at 3, keeping working thread beneath tip of needle; pull through gently. Swing thread in a clockwise direction and stitch down at 4 (to the right of, but in same hole as 3) and up at 5 (similarly next to 2), keeping thread beneath point of needle. Pull thread upward, then downward, until stitch is formed. Continue in same manner, working left to right.

 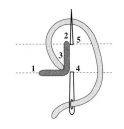 

  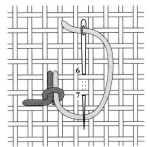 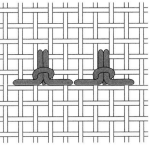

17. Bosnia Stitch

Make a series of vertical Straight Stitches (page 62) of equal height and equally spaced (1-2, 3-4, 5-6, etc.). Using the same or a contrast color, work diagonal Straight Stitches connecting the vertical stitches (A-B, C-D, E-F, etc.) to form a zigzag pattern. The diagonal stitches may be worked as shown or in the opposite diagonal direction (lower left to upper right).

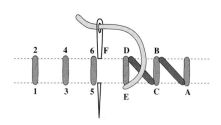

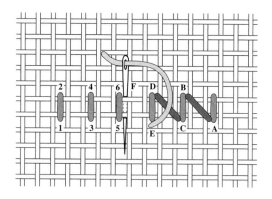

18. Bullion Knot

Come up at 1 and pull thread through. Stitch down at 2 and come up again at 1; do not pull needle completely through. Wrap working thread around top of needle several times (until length of twist equals the space between 1 and 2). Pull needle through (in direction shown by arrow) with non-stitching hand, while gently holding twist closely around needle with stitching hand. Stitch down at 2, pulling firmly to shape knot.

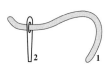

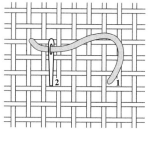
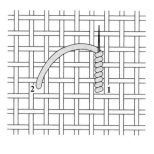

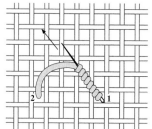
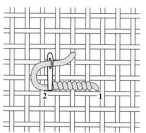

19. Buttonhole Stitch

Work as for Blanket Stitch (page 19), making stitches close together to fill the area.

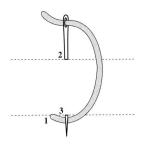

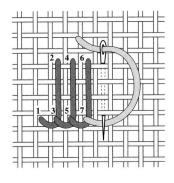

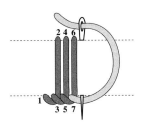

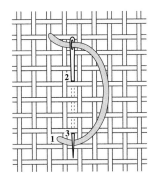

20. Buttonhole Stitch—Circular

This variation is made by working Buttonhole Stitches around a central hole of fabric. Begin as for Buttonhole Stitch (above), coming up at 1, down at 2 (center), up at 3 with loop underneath tip of needle and pull through. Working counterclockwise, make additional stitches, always entering fabric at center and coming out along the outside edge. To end, stitch down over final loop into same hole as 3.

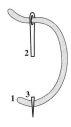

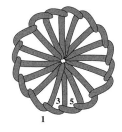

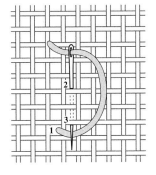

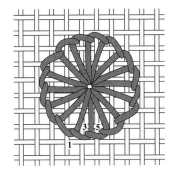

21. Buttonhole Stitch—Scalloped

Work Buttonhole Stitch (page 23), but increase, then decrease, the height of each stitch to form a repeat scallop pattern.

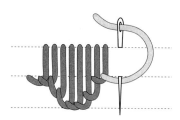

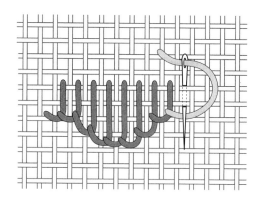

22. Cable Stitch

This stitch is worked from left to right along an imaginary line. Bring thread up at 1 and swing thread below line; stitch down at 2 and up at 3.

Swing thread above line and stitch down at 4 and up at 5. Continue in this manner, alternating the position of the thread; stitch down to end.

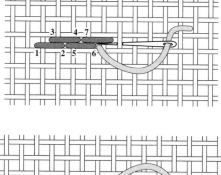

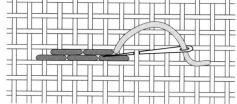

23. Chain Stitch

Bring thread up at 1. Form a counterclockwise loop and stitch down again at 2 (same hole as 1), holding loop with non-stitching thumb. Come up at 3, keeping loop beneath point of needle. Pull needle through, adjusting size and shape of loop. Repeat stitch to form a chain. End chain by stitching down over last loop at A. The chain can be worked horizontally, vertically, or along a curve.

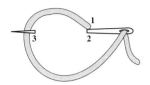

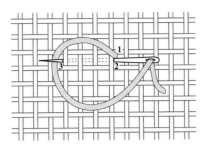

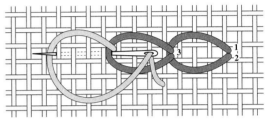

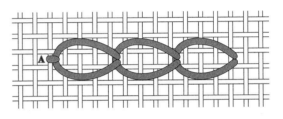

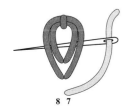

24. Chain Stitch—Braided

Make a small vertical stitch coming up at 1 and down at 2. Bring thread up at 3, pass needle under vertical (1-2) stitch without entering fabric and go down at 4 (same hole as 3). Come up at 5, pass needle under vertical stitch again, and go down at 6 (same hole as 5). Bring thread up at 7, pass needle under first two chains and go down at 8 (same hole as 7). Continue in same manner, working toward yourself. Stitch down to complete a chain at end.

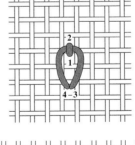

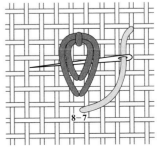

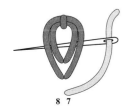

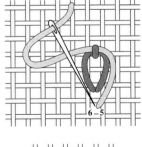

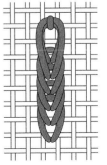

25. Chain Stitch—Cable

Bring thread up at 1 and form a clockwise loop. Wrap thread counterclockwise around needle and stitch down at 2 and up at 3, keeping loop beneath point of needle. Pull wrapped thread snug around needle, then pull needle through, adjusting size and shape of loop. Continue and end as for Chain Stitch (page 25).

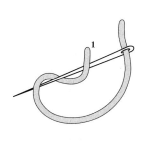

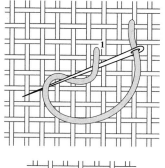

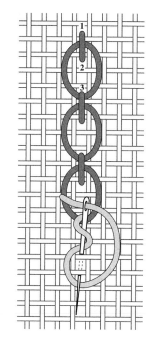

26. Chain Stitch—Lazy Daisy

Begin as for Chain Stitch (page 25), coming up at 1, down at 2 (same hole as 1), up at 3 keeping loop beneath point of needle. Pull through, adjusting loop to desired size, and stitch down at 4. Repeat desired number of petal shapes around the same central hole.

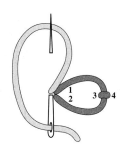
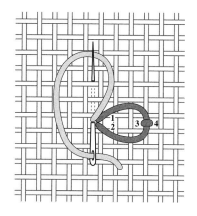

26

27. Chain Stitch—Open

This stitch is worked most comfortably toward yourself between two imaginary parallel lines. Bring thread up at 1. Swing thread counterclockwise and stitch down at 2 (across from 1) and up at 3 (below 1), keeping loop beneath point of needle. Pull needle through, adjusting size and shape of loop. Continue as for Chain Stitch (page 25), stitching down at 4, up at 5, etc. End chain by stitching down over each corner of last loop at A and B.

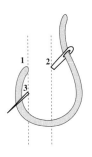
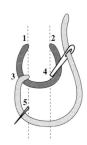
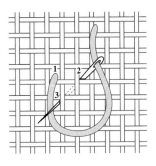
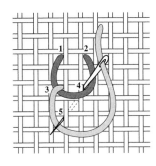

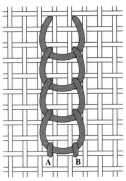

28. Chain Stitch—Rosette

Work this stitch from right to left between two imaginary parallel lines. Bring needle up at 1, form a counterclockwise loop, and go down at 2; emerge at 3 with loop beneath tip of needle. Pull needle through loop to desired shape and hold loop in place with thumb of non-stitching hand. To begin next stitch, pass needle under top right thread (to the left of 1) without entering fabric, form loop, and stitch down at 4, up at 5, etc. Stitch down to end last loop.

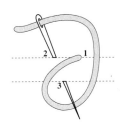
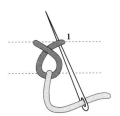
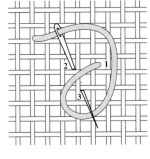
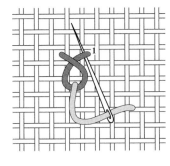

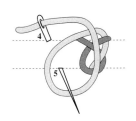
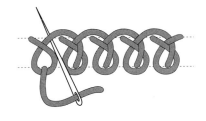
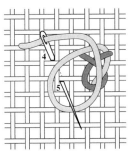
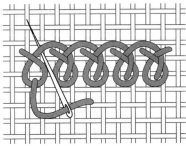

29. Chain Stitch—Twisted

Come up at 1 and form a counterclockwise loop; go down at 2 (to the left of 1) and up at 3 with loop beneath point of needle. Stitch down at 4 (to the left of 3 and outside of first loop) and form a new counterclockwise loop; come up at 5. Continue in this manner and end as for Chain Stitch.

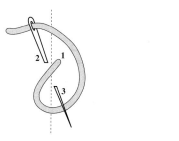 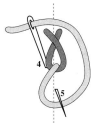  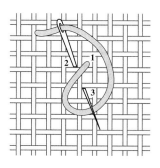 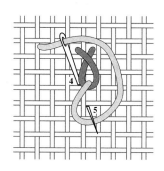

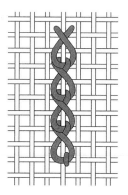 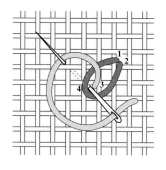

30. Chain Stitch—Zigzag

Begin as if for Chain Stitch (page 25). Make first link diagonally downward and second link diagonally upward. Continue in same manner and end as for Chain Stitch.

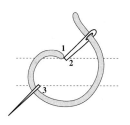 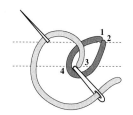 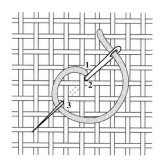

 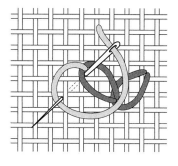

31. Chevron Stitch

This stitch is worked from left to right between two imaginary parallel lines. Begin on the lower line as if for Stem Stitch (page 61); bring thread up at 1, down at 2, and up at 3, pulling through with thread beneath point of needle. Move diagonally to upper line and stitch down at 4, up at 5; pull through.

Swing thread above work and stitch down at 6 and up at 7; pull through. Move diagonally to lower line and stitch down at 8, up at 9, down at 10, and up at 11, with thread beneath point of needle. Continue in this manner. Stitch down to end a completed horizontal stitch.

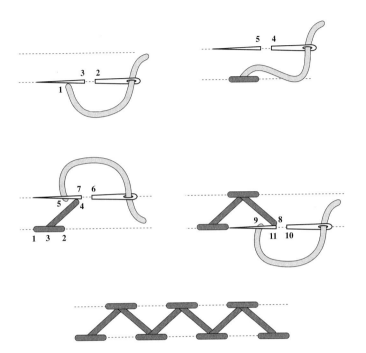

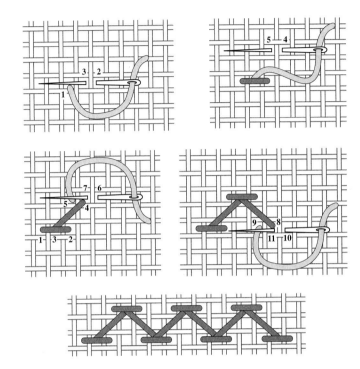

32. Colonial Knot

Come up at 1; swing thread in a clockwise loop and slip point of needle beneath beginning of loop. Wrap working thread around point of needle in a

figure eight motion. Insert needle at 2, one thread away from 1, and tighten wrap while pulling needle through to back of fabric.

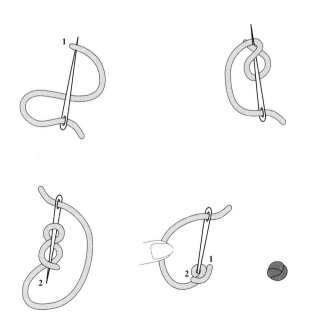

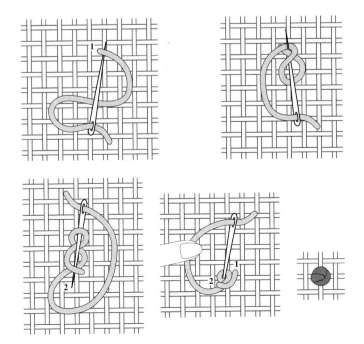

29

33. Coral Stitch

This stitch is made along an imaginary line, but can be worked in any direction or along a curve. Come up at 1 and make a counterclockwise loop, holding thread out toward the left. Stitch down at 2 (outside of loop) and up at 3 (just below 2 and inside of loop), with loop beneath point of needle. Pull through. Repeat and stitch down at end to anchor final knot.

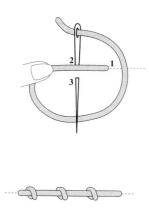

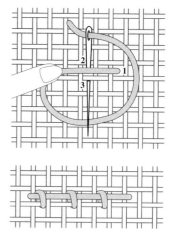

34. Coral Stitch—Zigzag

This stitch is worked from right to left between two imaginary parallel lines. Come up at 1, swing thread in a counterclockwise loop, and stitch down at 2, and up at 3; pull through to form first knot on upper line. Hold thread in a similar position and stitch down at 4 and up at 5, diagonally downward from first knot; pull through. Repeat on upper line and continue in a zigzag manner.

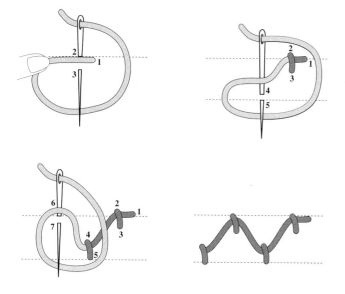

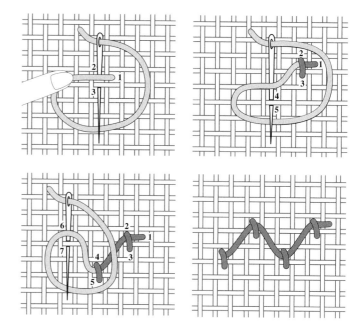

35. Couching

This stitch can be worked in any direction and along a curve. Bring thread up at 1, the beginning of the design line, and park the thread temporarily out of the way. Using a matching or contrasting thread, come up at A, down at B, up at C, etc., taking small stitches to hold or "couch" original thread in place. Stitch down at 2 to end couched thread.

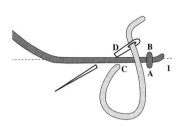

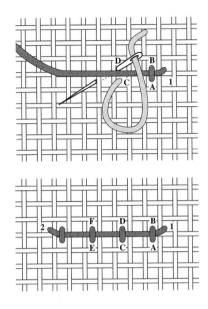

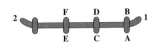

36. Couching—Bokhara

Rows of Couching (above) are worked close together to fill an area and the couching stitches form an additional pattern. Begin at the top of the area and Couch (A, B) each row below the previous one. Alternate placement of couching stitches to form desired pattern.

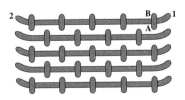

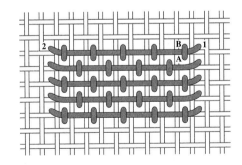

37. Cretan Stitch

This filling stitch is often worked in a leaf shape as shown. Begin with a small vertical stitch at tip (1-2). Come up at 3, swing thread to the right and stitch down at 4 and up at 5, with loop beneath point of needle and pull through; swing thread to the right again and stitch down at 6 and up at 7 in same manner. Swing thread to the left and stitch down at 8 and up at 9, etc. Continue in this manner, working each side from the outside edge toward center until shape is filled. Stitch down at center to end.

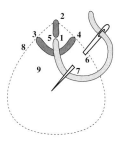
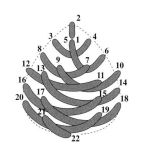
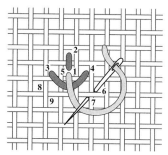
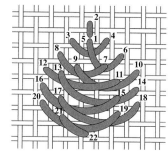

38. Cretan Stitch—Open

This open version of the Cretan Stitch (above) is usually worked from left to right rather than vertically like the closed version. It is worked between pairs of imaginary parallel lines. Bring thread up at 1, down at 2, and up at 3 (working toward yourself) with thread beneath point of needle; pull through. Stitch down at 4 and up at 5 (working away from yourself) with thread beneath point of needle; pull through. Repeat for desired length. Stitch down over loop to end.

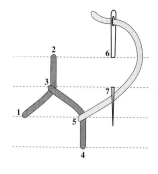
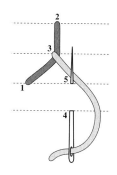
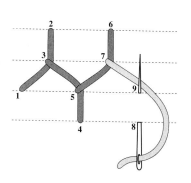
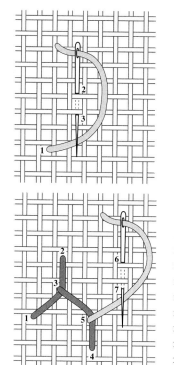
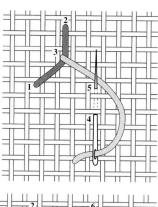
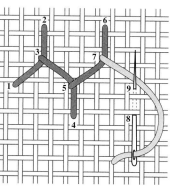

39. Cross Stitch

Bring thread up at 1, down at 2, up at 3, and down at 4 to make one complete stitch. When working a horizontal row of stitches, you can work the first half of each stitch (1-2) from left to right across the row, then work the second half of each stitch (3-4) from right to left.

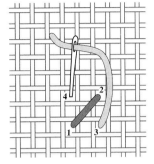

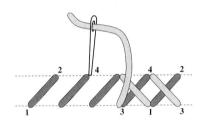

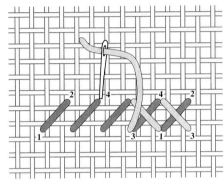

40. Cross Stitch—Double Upright

This variation of the Cross Stitch is worked individually. Begin as for Cross Stitch (above), making long 1-2 and 3-4 stitches. Now work a longer vertical (5-6) and a longer horizontal (7-8) stitch to create a diamond shape. Work horizontal rows left to right.

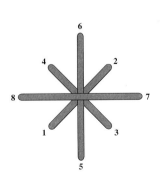

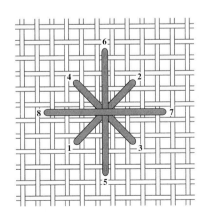

41. Cross Stitch—Long-Arm

Work this version of the Cross Stitch horizontally from left to right between two imaginary parallel lines. Begin each row with one Cross Stitch (page 33). Then bring thread up at 5 (same hole as 1) and stitch down at 6 and up at 7; pull through. Moving backward (to the left), stitch down at 8 (same hole as 2) and up at 9 (same hole as 3). Moving forward, stitch down at 10 and up at 11. Continue in this manner, ending with a backward stitch.

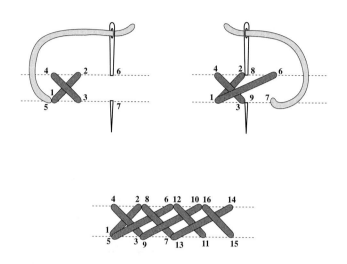

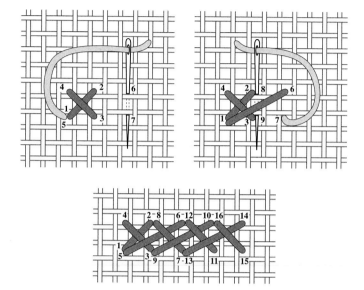

42. Cross Stitch—Oblong

Work as for Cross Stitch (page 33), making the stitches twice as high as they are wide. Each stitch can be worked individually as shown or work half of each stitch from left to right and complete each stitch on the return journey.

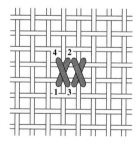

34

43. Cross Stitch—Reversible

Each of these stitches is completed before working the next one. Begin as for a Cross Stitch (page 33), coming up at 1 and down at 2. Make a second parallel stitch, coming up at 3 (same hole as 1) and down at 4 (same hole as 2). Come up at 5 and down at 6 to complete the stitch. The wrong side will also show a row of Cross Stitches, but they will separated by vertical stitches.

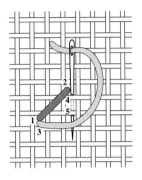

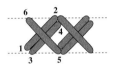

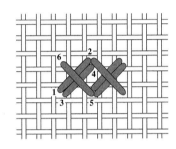

44. Cross Stitch—Smyrna

Begin as for Cross Stitch (page 33) making long 1-2 and 3-4 stitches, then make a vertical stitch (5-6) and a horizontal stitch (7-8) to create a square shape. Work horizontal rows from left to right.

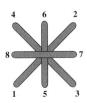

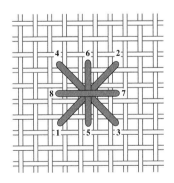

45. Cross Stitch—Tied

Each of these large stitches is completed before working the next one. Begin as for a Cross Stitch (page 33), coming up at 1, down at 2, up at 3 and down at 4. Work a center horizontal or vertical stitch by coming up at 5 and down at 6 to tie down the center of the stitch. Work rows from left to right.

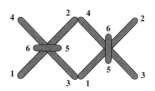

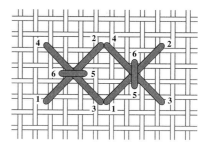

46. Cross Stitch—Upright

This variation consists of a vertical and a horizontal stitch that cross at their centers. Follow numerical sequence to complete each stitch. Work horizontal rows from left to right.

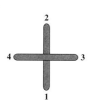

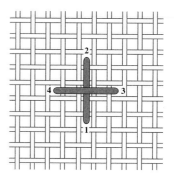

47. Eyelet Stitch

An Eyelet Stitch is made by bringing the thread up along the outside edge of a shape and stitching down at the center. Bring thread up at 1; follow the arrow and stitch down at the center of the shape. Come up at 2, again on the outside, and stitch down at center. Continue in this manner, working clockwise around the center, to fill the shape. If thread is slightly pulled after each downward stitch, a small hole will appear at the center of the eyelet.

48. Eyelet Stitch—Algerian

This variation, often called an Algerian Eye, is worked in the same manner as an Eyelet Stitch (page 36), but over a larger area. Follow numerical sequence, always stitching down at center. Do not pull too tightly on downward stitches. Work rows from left to right.

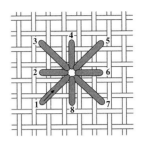

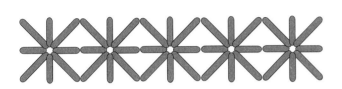

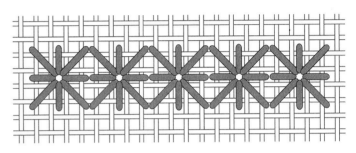

49. Eyelet Stitch—Diamond

Follow the numerical sequence to work an Eyelet Stitch (page 36), forming a diamond shape.

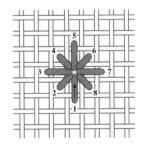

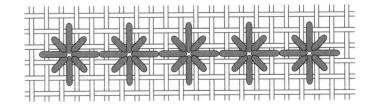

50. Eyelet Stitch—Half

Follow the numerical sequence to work the upper half of an Eyelet Stitch—Diamond (page 37) over a larger area. The lower half can be worked instead, if desired. Rows can be worked either from left to right or right to left.

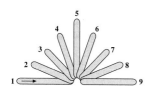

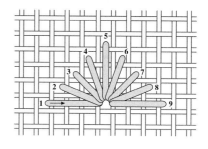

51. Feather Stitch

This stitch is worked between pairs of imaginary parallel lines. Come up at 1 and swing thread to the left. Stitch down at 2 (to the left of and even with 1) and up at 3 (below and between 1 and 2) with thread beneath point of needle; pull through. Swing thread to the right, stitch down at 4 and up at 5 with thread beneath point of needle; pull through. Continue in same manner, stitching down over last point of "V" shape to end sequence.

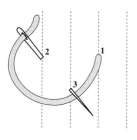

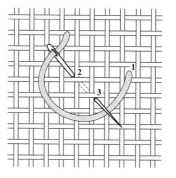

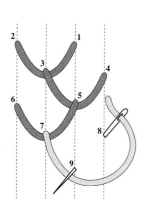

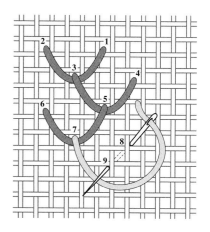

52. Feather Stitch—Chained

This version is also worked between pairs of imaginary parallel lines. Begin as for Chain Stitch (page 25), coming up at 1, down at 2. Move diagonally and come up at 3 with loop under point of needle and pull through. Continue in the same diagonal direction and stitch down at 4 to form an extended tie-down of the loop. Come up at 5 (to the left of 3), down at 6, up at 7, and pull through. Stitch down at 8 to form tie-down along the opposite diagonal. Continue in same manner, alternating diagonal directions, and end by stitching down over final loop.

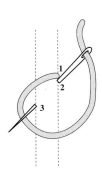

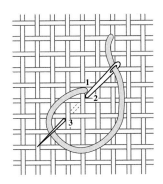

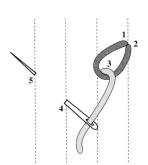

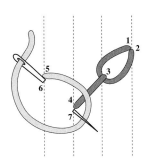

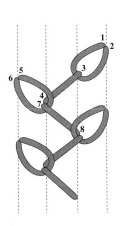

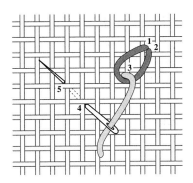

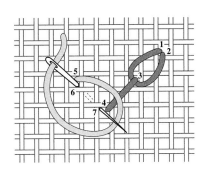

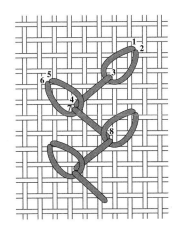

53. Feather Stitch—Closed

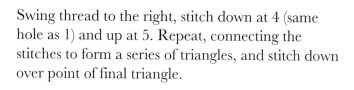

Begin as if for Feather Stitch (page 38), coming up at 1. After swinging thread to the left, stitch down at 2 (to the left of, but above 1) and up at 3 (below 2) with thread beneath point of needle; pull through.

Swing thread to the right, stitch down at 4 (same hole as 1) and up at 5. Repeat, connecting the stitches to form a series of triangles, and stitch down over point of final triangle.

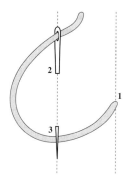

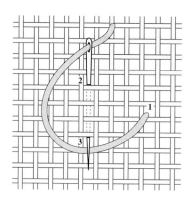

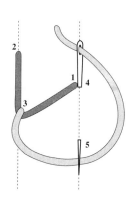

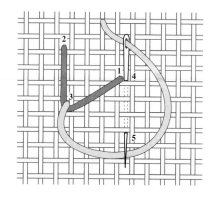

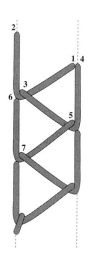

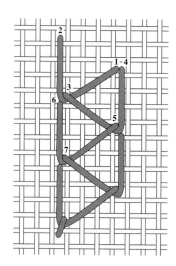

54. Feather Stitch—Double

This version is worked along imaginary parallel lines, but has an extra stitch worked on each side. Begin as for Feather Stitch (page 38), coming up at 1, then swing thread to the left. Continue to follow numerical sequence, swinging thread to the right for two stitches, then left for two stitches. End as for Feather Stitch.

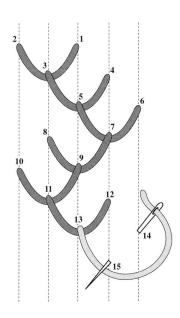

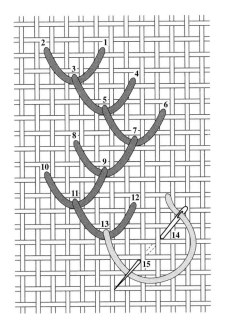

55. Fern Stitch

The Fern Stitch is made of three straight stitches that radiate from a central point; the center stitch is slightly longer than the side stitches. Bring thread up at 1, down at 2, up at 3 (same hole as 1), down at 4, up at 5 (same hole as 1), and down at 6 to complete the stitch. Continue, repeating sequence below previous group of three stitches.

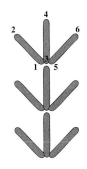

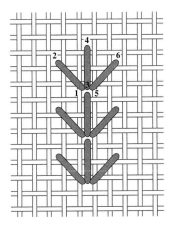

56. Fishbone Stitch

Bring thread up at 1 and stitch diagonally down at 2. Come up at 3 and pull through. Stitch down at 4 to complete the first stitch. For second stitch, come up at 5, down at 6, up at 7, and down at 8.

Continue in this manner to work a vertical row. Parallel vertical rows can be worked with sides of stitches sharing the same holes of the fabric.

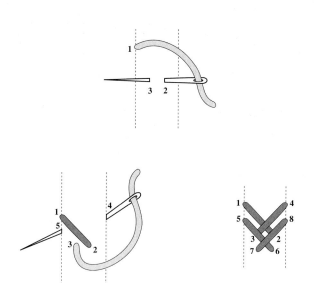

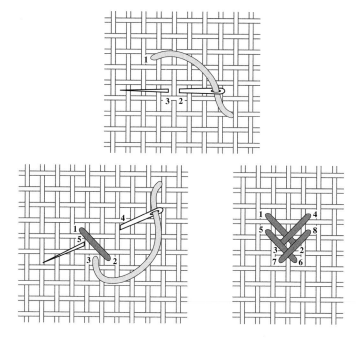

57. Fly Stitch

Bring thread up at 1 and swing thread to the right. Stitch down at 2 and up at 3 with thread beneath point of needle; pull through, forming a "V" shape.

Stitch down at 4. The stitches can be worked in rows (horizontal as shown or vertical) or in a random or repeat pattern.

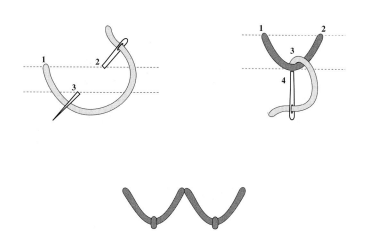

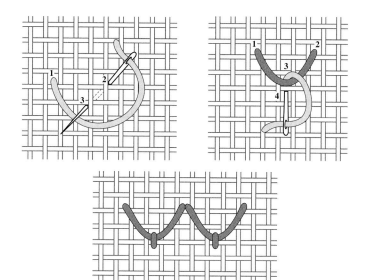

58. Fly Stitch—Extended

This variation is usually worked in vertical rows. Begin as for Fly Stitch (page 42), but work an extended tie-down (3-4) stitch. Work the second stitch by coming up at 5, swinging thread, stitching down at 6, up at 7 (same hole as 4), and down at 8. Continue in this manner. Extended Fly Stitches can also be worked in horizontal rows as shown with sides of stitches sharing the same holes of the fabric.

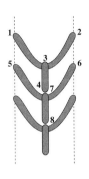
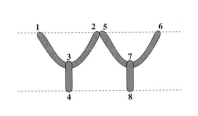
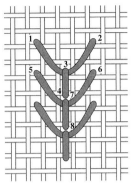
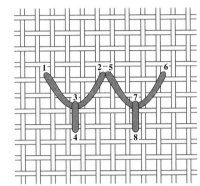

59. Four-Sided Stitch

Work horizontal rows from right to left. Bring thread up at 1, down at 2, up at 3, down at 4 (same hole as 1), up at 5, and down at 6 (same hole as 2) to form a backwards "C" shape. Begin sequence again, coming up at 7 (same hole as 3) and down at 8 (same hole as 5) to begin a new backwards "C" as the first square is enclosed. Continue in this manner, ending with a vertical stitch.

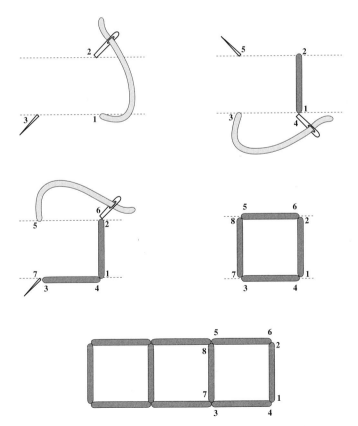
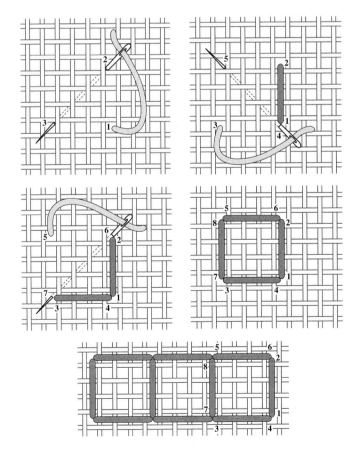

43

60. French Knot

Bring thread up at 1. Wrap thread once around shaft of needle. Insert needle at 2 (close to, but at least one thread away from 1). Pull wrapping thread snug around needle and hold the thread as needle is pulled through wrap; release floss as knot tightens. For a larger French Knot, use more strands of thread.

   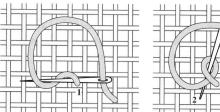 

61. Herringbone Stitch

This is worked from left to right between imaginary parallel lines. Bring thread up at 1. Stitch down at 2 and up at 3 along the upper line; pull through.

Stitch down at 4 and up at 5 along the lower line; pull through. Continue in this manner, stitching down to end along the lower line.

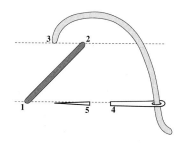

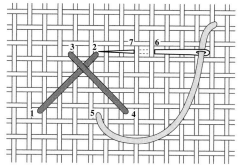

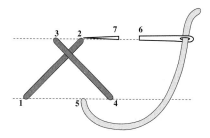

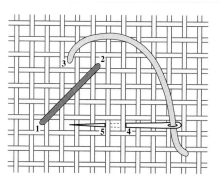

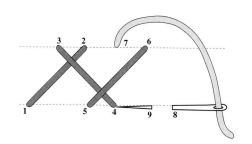

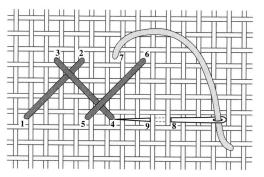

continued on next page

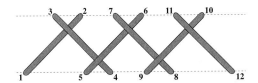

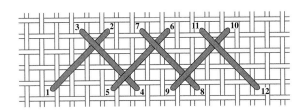

62. Herringbone Stitch—Closed

This variation is worked in the same manner as Herringbone Stitch (page 44), but the stitches are taller and more closely spaced. Follow numerical sequence to fill desired area.

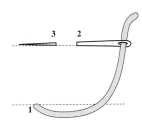

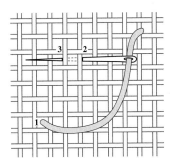

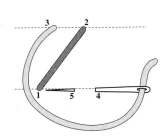

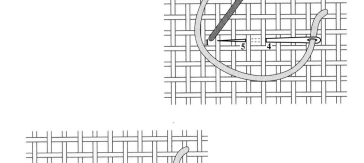

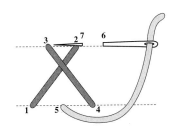

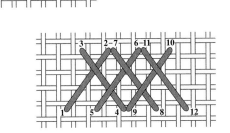

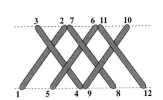

63. Herringbone Stitch—Tied

Work a row of Herringbone Stitches (page 44). Then, begin at the right and use the same or a contrasting thread to work a short vertical stitch (A, B) over each intersection.

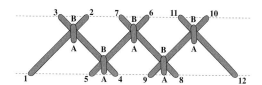

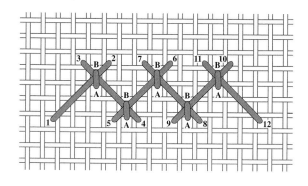

64. Interlaced Band

This stitch is worked between two imaginary parallel lines. Along each line, work a row of Backstitch (page 14); rows should be offset so the end of a stitch is opposite the center of a stitch in the other row. Using a matching or contrasting thread, come up at A and work an interlacing stitch between rows. Do not enter the fabric, just slip needle under each Backstitch. The needle should always be directed toward the center (between Backstitch rows) with the point over the working thread; stitch down to end work.

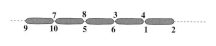

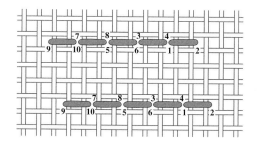

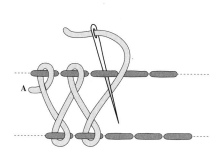

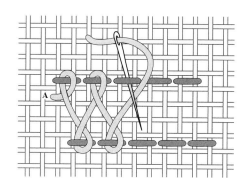

65. Knotted Stitch

This stitch is worked horizontally between two imaginary parallel lines; when counting threads, you must work over an uneven number of threads. Work a series of slanting stitches that are each tied down at the center. Bring thread up at 1, down at 2 to make the slanting stitch. Bring thread up at 3 and down at 4 to make a tiny stitch that ties down the center. Continue in this manner, working right to left.

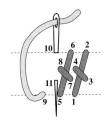 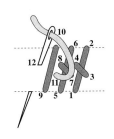 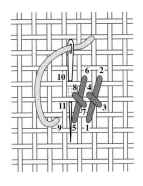 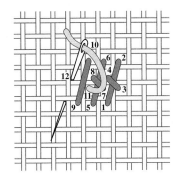

66. Lattice Stitch

This filling stitch is created by working long horizontal and vertical stitches, then anchoring the intersections with Cross Stitches (page 33).

Bring thread up at 1, down at 2, etc. to place long stitches in both directions. Using the same or a contrast color thread, make a Cross Stitch (A, B, C, D) over each intersection.

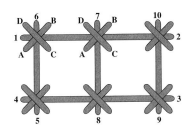 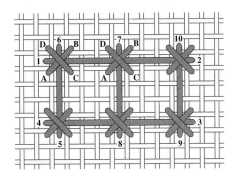

67. Leaf Stitch

This leaf shape is made with a series of stitches that radiate from a central imaginary line; the final stitch becomes the center vein. Follow numerical sequence to work counterclockwise around shape; bring thread up along outside edge and enter toward center. Anchor thread well on the back of work. Use the same or a contrast color for the final (A-B) stitch.

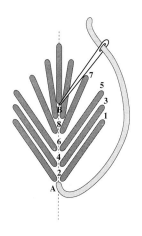

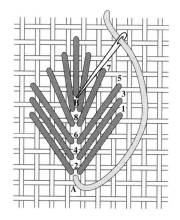

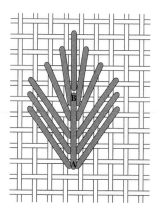

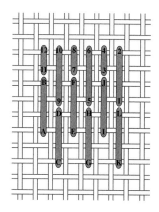

68. Long and Short Stitch

This technique is used to create shading in a desired area. Work the first row with alternating long and short stitches (1, 2, 3, etc.). Using a new shade of the same color, work the next (and all subsequent rows) with long stitches (A, B, C, etc). The effect is that of laying bricks. Stitch final row with long and short stitches to enclose area. If desired, you may split the thread of stitch above; refer to Backstitch—Split (page 14).

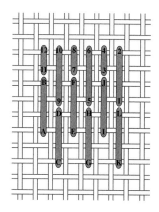

69. Loop Stitch

This stitch is worked along three imaginary parallel lines, with the middle line slightly closer to the lower line. Bring thread up at 1, down at 2, and up at 3. Make a clockwise loop. Slip needle beneath upper (1-2) stitch, with loop beneath point of needle; gently pull through to form a knot. Stitch down at 4, up at 5. Make loop and slip needle beneath stitch to form knot again. Repeat to desired length. End by stitching down after last knot.

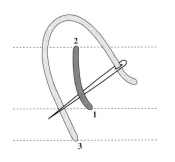

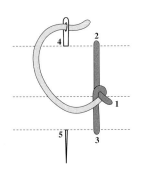

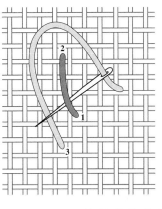

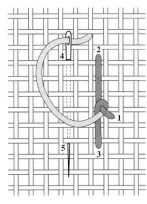

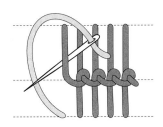

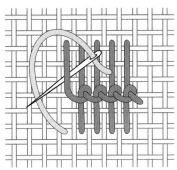

70. Maidenhair Stitch

This is worked between a series of imaginary parallel lines. It is similar to Feather Stitch (page 38) with a group of three stitches worked alternately on each side of the center. Bring thread up at 1 and swing thread to the left. Stitch down at 2 and up at 3 with thread beneath point of needle and pull through. Repeat, down at 4 and up at 5, then down at 6 and up at 7 with thread always beneath point of needle. Swing thread to the right and make three stitches on the opposite side. Continue in this manner, stitching down over last loop of thread.

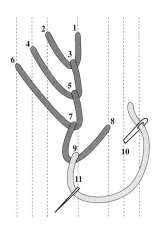

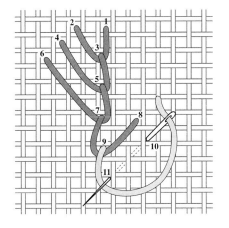

71. Montenegrin Stitch

This is similar to a Cross Stitch—Long-Arm (page 34), but has vertical stitches added to form a distinct pattern. Begin with a short sloping stitch, coming up at 1 and down at 2; make the vertical stitch (3-4), then cross the original stitch (5-6). Now begin the repeatable sequence, with a long sloping stitch (7-8), a vertical stitch (9-10) and a short crossing stitch (11-12). End sequence with an extra vertical stitch.

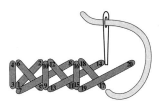

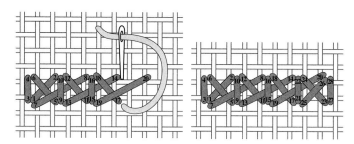

72. Palestrina Knot

This stitch is worked vertically between two imaginary parallel lines. Bring thread up at 1, down at 2, and up at 3; pull through. Slip needle from right to left (A) under the first (1-2) stitch without entering fabric and pull through. Make a counter-clockwise loop and again slip needle (B) under the first stitch with loop beneath point of needle; pull through to form knot. Continue in same manner and stitch down after final knot.

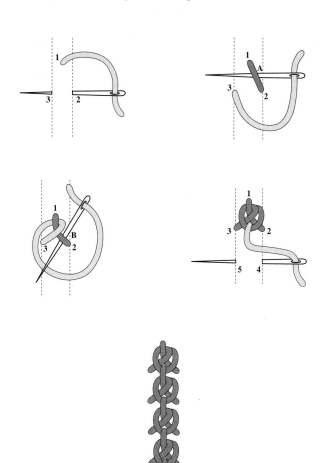
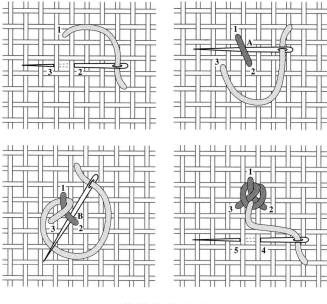
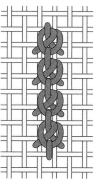

73. Parma Stitch

This is a combination of Chain Stitch (page 25) and Blanket Stitch (page 19). Begin by working three adjacent rows of Chain Stitch from left to right; make sure the links are aligned across all three rows. Now bring thread up at beginning of middle row (A) and work Blanket Stitch by slipping thread beneath the inner edges of the first and second row of Chain Stitch; do not enter fabric. Work two (or more) Blanket Stitches in each pair of links. Stitch down at end of row. Turn work top to bottom, bring thread up at B, and repeat the Blanket Stitch sequence joining the remaining inner edges. The final effect will have the Blanket Stitch knots along the center with the "legs" pointing toward the outside edges.

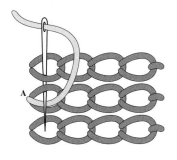

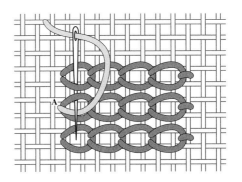

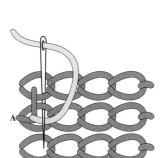

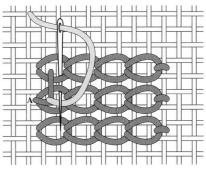

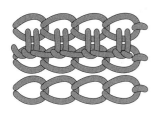

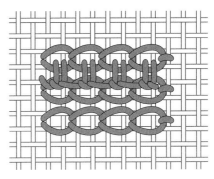

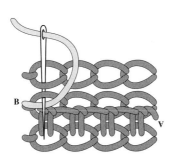

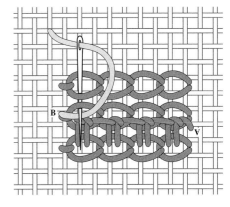

74. Pattern Darning

The technique of Pattern Darning is similar to working several rows of Running Stitch (page 57). Come up at 1, down at 2, etc., working the desired distance to fill a space. Make slightly longer stitches on the surface of the fabric and shorter stitches beneath the fabric, so more thread is visible than for Running Stitch. On the second (and subsequent) row(s), alter the placement of the stitches to create a pattern. There are endless variations in Pattern Darning, determined by stitch length and row position.

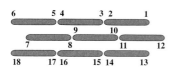

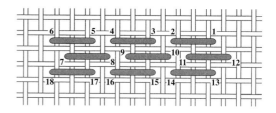

75. Pekinese Stitch

This is a laced variation of the Backstitch. Work a row of Backstitch (page 14) from right to left. Using the same or a contrasting thread, come up at A (below stitch at left end of row), swing thread to the right and slip needle upward under second stitch (B) without entering fabric, and downward under first stitch (C). Pull through to form desired size loop. Repeat sequence (up at D, down at E, pull through) to form second and subsequent loops. To end, stitch down below center of last Backstitch.

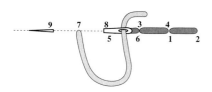

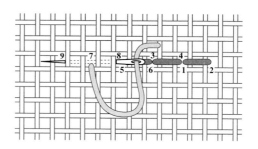

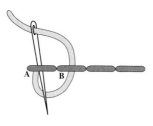

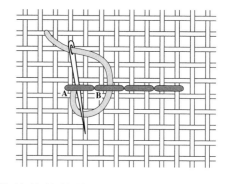

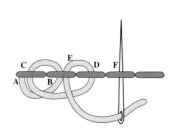

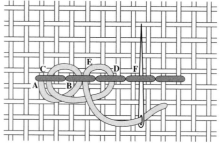

76. Pistil Stitch

Bring needle up at 1 and wrap working thread twice around shaft of needle. Swing point of needle clockwise and reinsert at 2, desired distance from 1.

Pull wrapping thread around needle and hold with thumb and forefinger of non-stitching hand while pulling needle through to back of fabric.

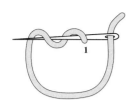

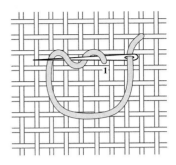

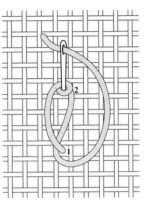

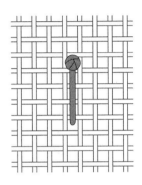

77. Queen Stitch

This forms a diamond shape on the fabric. Bring thread up at 1 and down at 2 to make a long, loose vertical stitch. Come up at 3 and down at 4 to anchor center of first stitch out toward right side. Make a similar stitch (up at 5, down at 6, up at 7, down at 8) for the second stitch on the right side. On the left side, make the third (9, 10, 11, 12) and fourth (13, 14, 15, 16) stitches out toward the left side to complete the sequence.

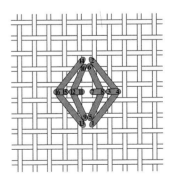

78. Raised Chain Band

Work a series of equally spaced horizontal Straight Stitches (page 62), coming up at 1, down at 2, etc. Using the same or a contrasting thread, come up at A, above center of first stitch. Swing thread clockwise and slip needle upward under first stitch (B), without entering fabric; pull through. Swing thread counterclockwise and slip needle downward under first stitch (C) and pull through to form knot. Repeat (up at D, down at E) to form a knot on each Straight Stitch. End by stitching down over last loop.

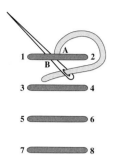

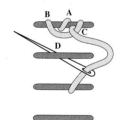

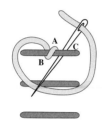

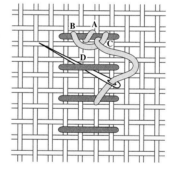

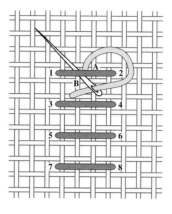

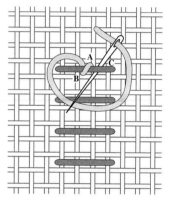

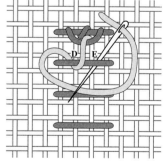

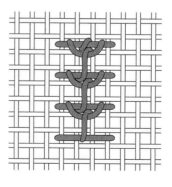

54

79. Ray Stitch

This series of nine stitches fills a square area of fabric. Bring thread up at 1 (bottom right corner) and stitch down at bottom left corner, making a horizontal stitch. Bring thread up at 2 (directly above 1) and stitch down again at bottom left corner. Follow numerical sequence around square, always entering fabric at the same corner. The fifth stitch is the diagonal corner one.

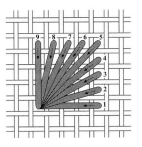

80. Rhodes Stitch

This series of stitches fills a square area, but all stitches are worked from one side of the square to the other to produce a raised center. The last stitch will be a corner diagonal one. Bring thread up at 1 (just above the bottom left corner) and stitch down at 2 (just below top right corner), up at 3, etc. Complete the square with the final (19-20) stitch.

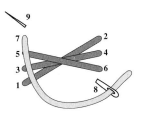

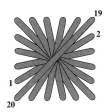

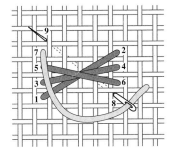

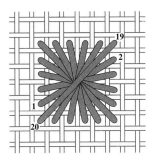

81. Rice Stitch

Make a large Cross Stitch (page 33), coming up at 1, down at 2, up at 3, and down at 4. Using the same or a contrasting thread, tie down each of the four corners with a small stitch. The sequence is similar to Backstitch (page 14), moving in a counterclockwise direction. Come up at A, down at B, up at C, etc., to complete the stitch.

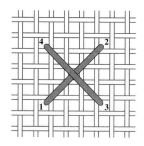

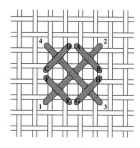

82. Roumanian Stitch

This stitch is worked vertically between two imaginary parallel lines. Bring thread up at 1 and down at 2 to make a horizontal stitch; pull through. Come up at 3 (above and to the right of center of stitch) and down at 4 (below and to the left of center of stitch). Repeat this sequence directly below first stitch, and continue in this manner to fill desired space.

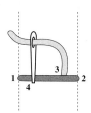

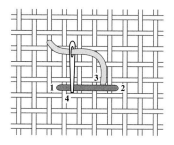

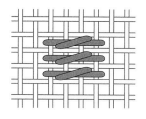

83. Running Stitch

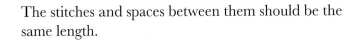

This stitch is worked along an imaginary line. Bring thread up at 1, down at 2, up at 3, down at 4, etc.

The stitches and spaces between them should be the same length.

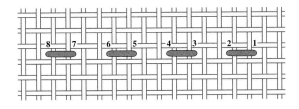

84. Running Stitch—Double

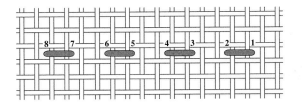

Work a row of Running Stitch (above). At end of row, follow the alphabetical sequence to work a row in the opposite direction, filling the spaces

between the previously made stitches. The wrong side will look the same as the right side

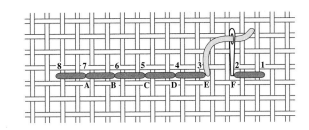

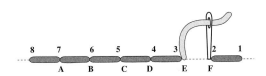

85. Running Stitch—Interlaced

Work a row of Running Stitch (page 57). Using the same or a contrasting thread, come up at A, slip needle downward under second stitch at B and pull through gently to form a curve. Do not enter fabric.

Slip needle upward under third stitch at C, downward at D, etc. At end of row, return and work from left to right to complete each loop. Stitch down under last Running Stitch to end.

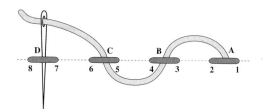

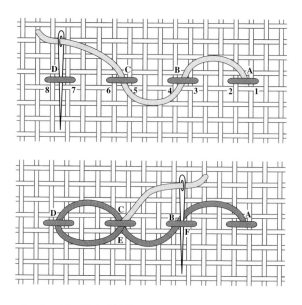

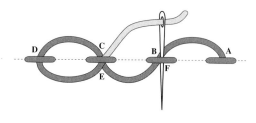

86. Satin Stitch

Follow the numerical sequence to work Straight Stitches (page 62) next to each other to fill the desired space. Satin Stitch can be worked vertically, horizontally, or diagonally, and can be used to fill any desired shape. Do not make stitches too long or they might snag.

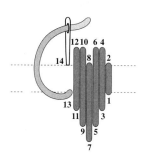

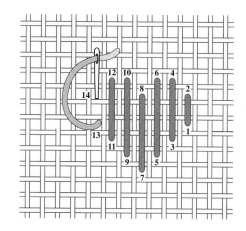

87. Scroll Stitch

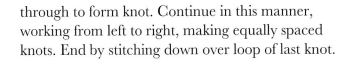

Come up at 1. Form a clockwise loop and stitch down at 2 and up at 3, making a small stitch inside of loop. Pull working thread to tighten loop around needle. Hold tightened loop and pull needle through to form knot. Continue in this manner, working from left to right, making equally spaced knots. End by stitching down over loop of last knot.

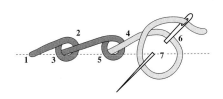

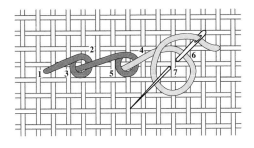

88. Sheaf Stitch

This compact stitch is made from three vertical Straight Stitches (page 62) that are tied down by two small horizontal stitches. Bring thread up at 1, down at 2, up at 3, etc., pulling through gently for each stitch. Bring thread up at 7 (just above and to the left of center) and slip needle beneath the three vertical stitches (A), gathering them together; do not enter fabric. Slip the needle beneath the group again (B) to form the second horizontal stitch. Stitch down at 8 to end. The stitches can be worked alternately to form a pattern or adjacent to each other in horizontal or vertical rows.

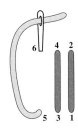

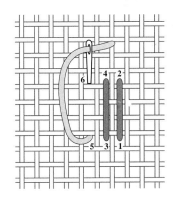

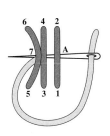

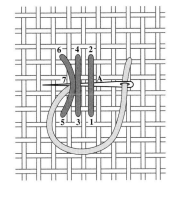

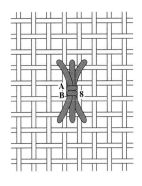

89. Shell Stitch

This is similar to the Sheaf Stitch (page 59), but is slightly larger and connected with a series of loops. Bring thread up at 1, down at 2, etc., pulling through gently each time. Come up at 9 and down at 10 to gather and tie down the vertical stitches.

Continue to form a row. Using a contrasting or the same thread, interlace the 9-10 gathering stitches as for Running Stitch—Interlaced (page 58). If desired, the interlacing can be worked a second time for a bulkier effect.

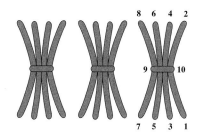

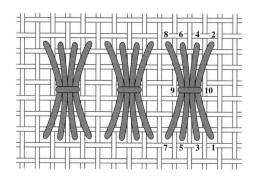

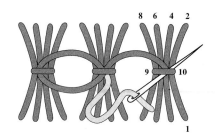

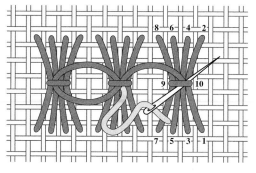

90. Spider Web

This stitch is made within an imaginary circle. Begin by making a Fly Stitch—Extended (page 43). Add two extra spokes (5-6 and 7-8) to create a base for the web. Bring the same (or a contrasting) thread up at center (A) and begin weaving over and under

the five spokes in a spiral manner until desired fullness is achieved; do not enter fabric. To end, stitch down beneath center of web. Larger webs can be made with longer and/or more spokes, always of an uneven number.

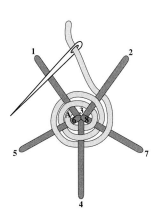

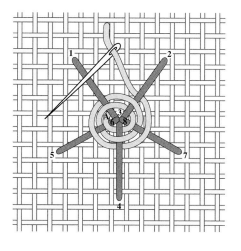

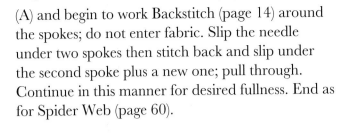

91. Spider Web—Backstitched

This version can be made with an uneven or an even number of spokes and this kind of weaving produces a ridged effect. Make desired number of spokes with evenly spaced Straight Stitches (page 62) across an imaginary circle (1-2, 3-4, 5-6, 7-8). Bring the same (or a contrasting) thread up at center

(A) and begin to work Backstitch (page 14) around the spokes; do not enter fabric. Slip the needle under two spokes then stitch back and slip under the second spoke plus a new one; pull through. Continue in this manner for desired fullness. End as for Spider Web (page 60).

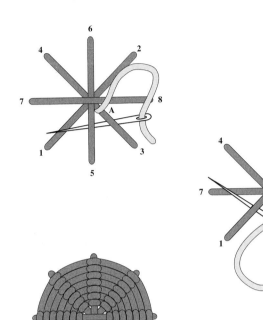

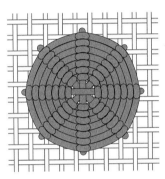

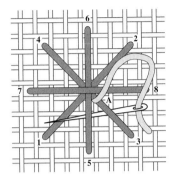

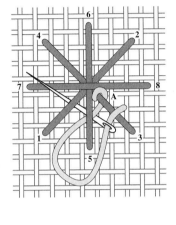

92. Stem Stitch

Bring thread up at 1, along an imaginary line. Hold thread below line with the thumb of your non-stitching hand. Stitch down at 2 and up at 3 (half way between 1 and 2); pull through. Continue in this manner with the working thread always below the imaginary line. You can also work with the

thread always above your work, and this is usually called Outline Stitch (not shown). Work straight or curved rows; when working on a tight curve, change position of working thread so it is on the outside of the curve.

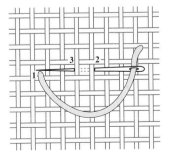

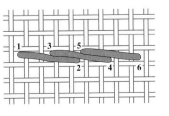

93. Stem Stitch—Portuguese

Begin as for Stem Stitch (page 61), coming up at 1, down at 2, and up at 3; pull through. Make a clockwise loop and slip the needle under the stitch just made (A), not entering fabric. Toward the left, slip the needle again under same stitch (B) and pull through. Continue making Stem Stitches (down at 4 and up at 5), then wrapping the stitch twice (A, B). End by stitching down after second wrap.

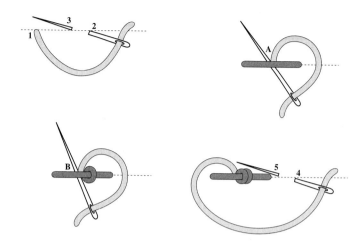

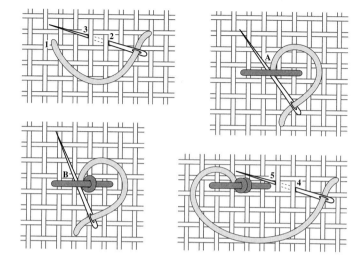

94. Straight Stitch

Bring thread up at 1 and down at 2. Straight Stitches can be worked in different directions, of varying sizes, and spaced as desired. Straight Stitches can be used to fill out or compensate a small area composed of other stitches.

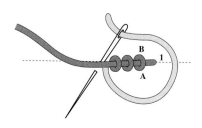

95. Trailing Stitch

This is similar to Couching, but creates a tightly coiled appearance. Begin as for Couching (page 31), coming up at 1; park first thread temporarily out of the way. Using a matching or contrasting thread, come up at A, down at B, up at C, etc., making small stitches next to each other to form a continuous coiling line. Stitch down at end of design line to end couched thread and coiling thread.

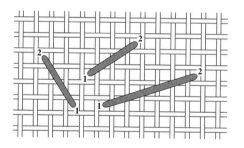

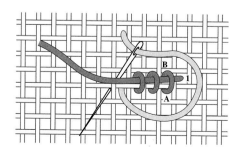

96. Trellis Stitch

This stitch can be used to fill any desired space. Come up at 1, down at 2, up at 3, etc. to work diagonal Straight Stitches (page 62) in one direction; repeat in the opposite direction. Stitches should be evenly spaced. Using the same or a contrasting thread, come up at A and down at B to anchor each intersection of diagonal threads. The area to be filled is usually outlined with another stitch such as Backstitch—Split (page 14), Chain Stitch (page 25), or Stem Stitch (page 61). The intersections can also held in place with beads (pages 17 and 18).

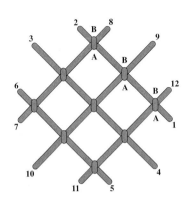

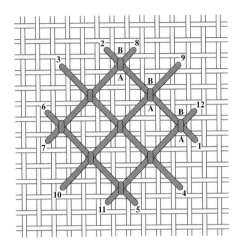

97. Triangle Stitch

This stitch is made in two journeys, the first from left to right and the second from right to left. Work along three imaginary parallel lines. Bring thread up at 1 and down at 2 to make a short vertical stitch. Come up at 3 (same hole as 1) and down at 4 to make a long diagonal stitch. Continue for desired distance. On the return journey, bring thread up at A and down at B for the diagonal stitch, and up at C (same hole as A) and down at D for the vertical stitch to complete each triangle.

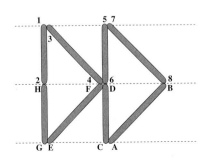

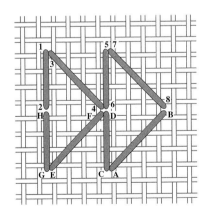

98. Turkey Work

Looped stitches are made then trimmed to form a cut pile. Begin on the top of the fabric and stitch down at 1, leaving the thread end free on the surface, and come up at 2 (to the left of 1); pull through. Swing thread below work and stitch down at 3 and up at 4 (same hole as 1); pull through to anchor beginning of row. Swing thread above work, stitch down at 5 and up at 6 (same hole as 3); pull partially through, leaving a loop on fabric surface.

Swing thread below work and stitch down at 7 and up at 8; pull through to anchor loop. Repeat to end of row and stitch down to anchor last loop. Push row of loops upward. Begin second row below first row and work left to right again. Repeat rows to fill desired area. Cut each row of loops so pile is of consistent height. For a lacy effect the Turkey Work can be left uncut as shown in our photographed samples.

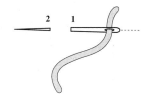

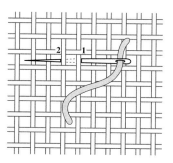

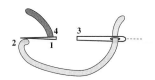

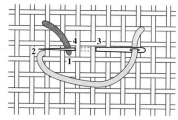

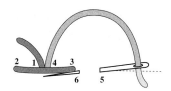

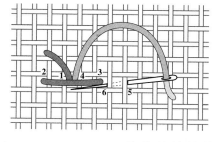

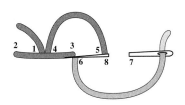

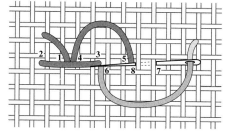

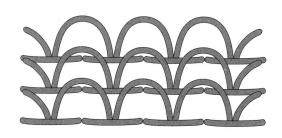

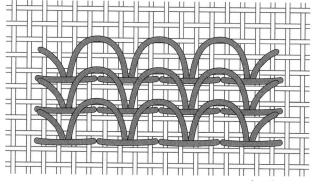

continued on next page

64

Turkey Work *continued*

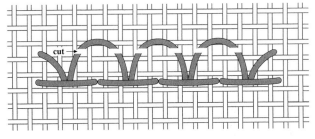

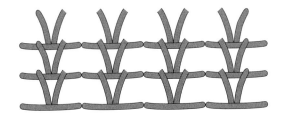

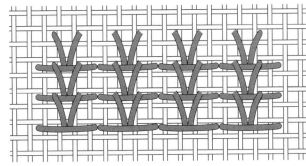

99. Vandyke Stitch

This stitch is worked vertically between two imaginary parallel lines. Bring thread up at 1, down at 2, up at 3 (to the left of and even with 2); pull through. Stitch down at 4 and up at 5 (just below 1); pull through. Slip needle beneath crossed threads from right to left, not entering fabric. Stitch down at 6 and up at 7; pull through. Slip needle under crossed threads and continue in same manner for desired length. Stitch down at right side to end.

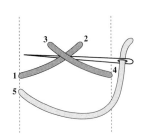

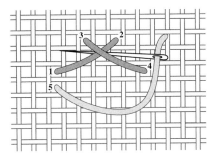

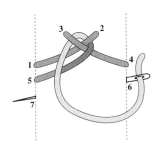

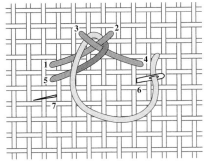

100. Wave Stitch

This stitch is worked with horizontal rows in alternating directions to fill an area. Work the first row from right to left. Bring thread up at 1, down at 2, and up at 3; pull through. Stitch down at 4 (same hole as 1) and up at 5; pull through. Repeat to end of row. Work second row from left to right. Bring thread up at A, down at B, and up at C; pull through. Stitch down at D (same hole as A) and up at E; pull through. Repeat rows to fill desired area.

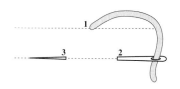

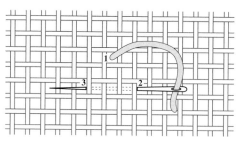

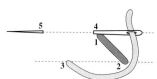

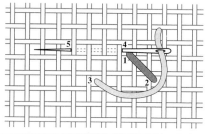

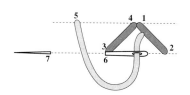

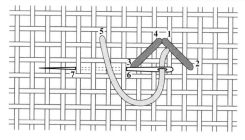

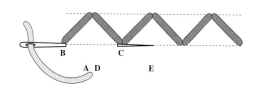

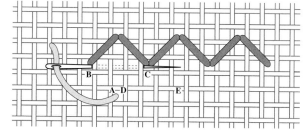

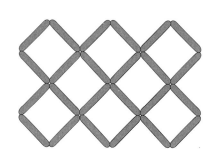

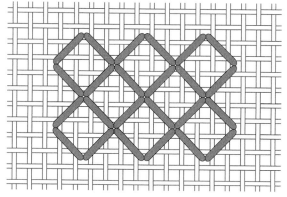

101. Wheat Ear Stitch

This stitch is worked vertically along three imaginary parallel lines. Bring thread up at 1 and down at 2, up at 3, and down at 4 (same hole as 2), to make two diagonal stitches. Come up at 5 and slip needle from right to left (A) beneath the two

diagonal stitches (not entering fabric); stitch down at 6 (same hole as 5) and pull through, adjusting loop to desired size. Repeat the sequence for desired number of stitches.

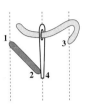

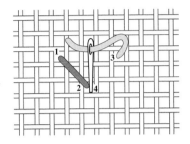

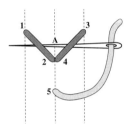

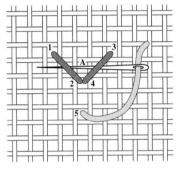

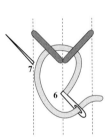

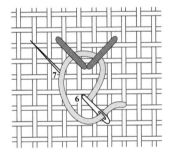

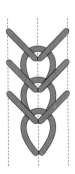

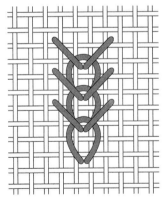

Index of Stitches